D1274691

POLAR BEARS
OF THE ARCTIC

SARA SWAN MILLER

PowerKiDS press.
New York

Published in 2009 by The Rosen Publishing Group, Inc.
29 East 21st Street, New York, NY 10010

First Edition

Editor: Amelie von Zumbusch
Book Design: Kate Laczynski
Photo Researcher: Jessica Gerweck

Photo Credits: Back cover (caribou) © www.istockphoto.com/Paul Loewen; back cover (emperor penguins) © www.istockphoto.com/Bernard Breton; back cover, cover, p. 1 © www.istockphoto.com/Michel de Nijs; back cover (seals), pp. 4, 8, 10, 14 Shutterstock.com; back cover (walruses) © Getty Images; back cover (whales) © Paul Nicklen/Getty Images; p. 6 © www.istockphoto.com/David T. Gomez; p. 12 © Wayne Lynch/Age Fotostock; p. 16 © Tom Soucek/Age Fotostock; p. 18 © Grambo/Getty Images; p. 20 © Kevin Spreekmeester/Age Fotostock.

Library of Congress Cataloging-in-Publication Data

Miller, Sara Swan.
   Polar bears of the Arctic / Sara Swan Miller. — 1st ed.
      p. cm. — (Brrr! polar animals)
   Includes index.
   ISBN 978-1-4358-2741-7 (library binding) — ISBN 978-1-4358-3145-2 (pbk.)
ISBN 978-1-4358-3151-3 (6-pack)
   1. Polar bear—Arctic regions—Juvenile literature. I. Title.
   QL737.C27M513 2009
   599.786—dc22
                                        2008023680

Manufactured in the United States of America

CONTENTS

Though a polar bear's thick coat makes the bear look white, the skin underneath it is black.

REALLY BIG BEARS

Polar bears are huge! They are the world's largest meat-eating land animals. Male polar bears are 8 to 10 feet (2.4–3 m) from nose to tail. Females are a bit smaller. They are 6 to 8 feet (2–2.4 m) long. They are still very big bears! Polar bears are heavy, too. The largest polar bear ever seen was a male that weighed a whopping 2,209 pounds (1,002 kg).

Polar bears look white. In fact, the hairs of a polar bear's coat are clear and **hollow**. They **reflect** light, making the bears look white. This makes polar bears hard to spot against the snow.

These polar bears are crossing the ice of the Hudson Bay near Cape Churchill, Canada. More than half of the world's polar bears live in Canada.

6

WHERE ARE THE POLAR BEARS?

Polar bears live in the Arctic, which is the area around the North Pole. There is plenty of snow and ice there year-round. This is why the bears need white-looking fur all year.

How would you find polar bears? You would have to travel to the cold coasts of Alaska, Canada, Russia, Greenland, or Norway. The bears live in places where they can hunt for seals in the open water. Polar bears often ride on **ice floes** way out into the open sea. An ice floe is a big chunk of ice that floats in the water.

*Polar bears often rest to keep from getting overheated, or too hot.
They also sometimes eat snow to cool down.*

STAYING WARM

It gets very cold in the Arctic. Polar bears can stay warm, though. Their bodies are covered with two **layers** of fur. Even their feet are covered with thick fur. Under their coats, polar bears have a thick layer of fat. This fat may be 4 inches (10 cm) thick!

Its fur and fat keep a polar bear's heat trapped close to its body. Its tail and ears are small, which keeps the bear from losing heat to the outside air. In fact, polar bears are so well **protected** from the cold that they sometimes get too hot! Therefore, they move slowly and rest often.

Polar bears are wonderful swimmers. In fact, many people consider these bears to be marine, or ocean, animals.

SUPER SWIMMERS

Polar bears spend a lot of time in the water, and they are great swimmers. Their long bodies help them slip through the water. The fat under their skin helps them float. Polar bears use their large, flat feet like oars. They paddle with their front paws and **steer** with their back paws. **Webbing** between their toes helps them swim even faster.

Polar bears can swim for hours without stopping. They can swim as far as 60 miles (100 km) at a time. Polar bears are also good at diving deep under water to hunt. They can hold their breath for 2 minutes.

This polar bear has caught a bearded seal. Ringed seals and bearded seals are the kinds of seals that polar bears eat most often.

YUMMY SEALS

Seals are a polar bear's most-liked food. A polar bear often waits at a seal's breathing hole for the seal to come up for air. Then the bear charges at the seal. Other times, a bear will wait on the edge of an ice floe for a seal to swim by. Then the bear dives down after the seal. In the spring, bears sometimes dig into seal dens where mothers are caring for their pups. The pups make a fine meal.

Bears eat walruses and small whales, too. They even eat reindeer and birds. Sometimes, the bears break into **garbage** dumps for fine feasts.

These polar bears have come together to feed on a sperm whale that washed up on a rocky beach.

ALONE AND TOGETHER

Many meat-eating **mammals** hunt together in packs. However, polar bears do not. They spend most of the year hunting, eating, and sleeping alone. Springtime is different, though. Males search for females with which to **mate**. The bears' very good sense of smell helps them find their mates. At mating time, the males fight over the females.

Polar bears also sometimes come together to eat. Every so often, several polar bears find a feast of dead whale or walrus. They share it without fighting over it. As many as 40 polar bears may gather around to eat a big whale.

16 Polar bear cubs first leave their dens in March or April. By that time, they are already a few months old.

POLAR BABIES

A female that is going to be a mother spends the summer and fall months eating a lot. She will need lots of stored fat to get her through the months that she will spend in her den with her cubs.

The soon-to-be mother digs a den in the snow in the late fall. She gives birth to one to three cubs in December or January. The mother stays in the den with the cubs and feeds them with her milk. Her milk is very high in fat. This gives the cubs a lot of **energy** and helps them stand the cold.

Mother polar bears take very good care of their young. They will even put their own lives in danger to keep their babies safe.

GROWING UP

When they are born, polar bear cubs weigh only about 21 ounces (600 g). Thanks to their mother's rich milk, though, they grow quickly. By late March, they weigh about 12 pounds (5 kg). Now, they are ready to leave the den with their mother. By this point, the mother is very hungry. She has not eaten for over three months! The cubs travel with their mother as she goes hunting for food.

Polar bear cubs stay with their mother for over two years. She protects them and teaches them how to hunt. Then, they are ready to go off on their own.

Today, polar bears are not generally killed if they get in the way of people. Instead, they are caught and moved back to the wild.

POLAR BEARS AND PEOPLE

Full-grown polar bears have no enemies except people. For thousands of years, Arctic people have hunted these bears. The people of the Arctic use polar bears for food and clothing. Polar bear skins make warm blankets or comfy rugs, too. These bears have always been part of Arctic people's lives.

However, other people discovered polar bears and began hunting them a few hundred years ago. They sold polar bear skins to make money. People began to worry that too many bears were being killed. Today, polar bears are protected by law. People may not kill them from **helicopters** or large motorboats.

POLAR BEARS IN TROUBLE

Even with the new laws, there are fewer polar bears. Oil spills are one reason for this. When polar bears become covered with oil, their fur can no longer keep them warm.

The bears' biggest problem is that the world is warming up. This means the Arctic's ice is melting. Polar bears have to swim much farther out to find seals to eat. The bears are great swimmers, but these long swims can be too much for them. Bears have even drowned while swimming. People are trying to keep the world from warming up, though. If we all work together, we can save this wonderful animal!

GLOSSARY

energy (EH-nur-jee) The power to work or to act.

garbage (GAHR-bij) Things that are thrown away.

helicopters (HEH-luh-kop-terz) Aircraft that are kept in the air by blades that spin above the craft.

hollow (HOL-oh) Having a hole through the center.

ice floes (EYES FLOHZ) Large, flat pieces of floating ice.

layers (LAY-erz) Thicknesses of something.

mammals (MA-mulz) Warm-blooded animals that have backbones and hair, breathe air, and feed milk to their young.

mate (MAYT) To come together to make babies.

protected (pruh-TEKT-ed) Kept safe.

reflect (rih-FLEKT) To throw back light, heat, or sound.

steer (STEER) To guide something's path.

webbing (WEB-bing) Skin between the toes that animals use to swim.

INDEX

WEB SITES

Due to the changing nature of Internet links, PowerKids Press has developed an online list of Web sites related to the subject of this book. This site is updated regularly. Please use this link to access the list:
www.powerkidslinks.com/brrr/pbear/